A Simple Guide to Self-Publishing

A time and money-saving handbook to printing, distributing and promoting your own book.

A WISE OWL BOOK

A Simple Guide to Self-Publishing
Copyright © 1994 by Mark Ortman
All rights reserved

Cover design: Linda Ruljancich

ISBN 0-9634699-8-3

Library of Congress Catalog Card Number: 93-61767

Manufactured in the United States
10 9 8 7 6 5 4 3 2 1

WISE OWL BOOKS
P.O. Box 621
Kirkland WA 98083
(206) 822-9699

The suggestions outlined in this book are not intended to substitute legal, accounting or other professional services. If expert assistance is required, the services of a competent professional should be sought.

Acknowledgments

A special thanks to all the people who helped make this book possible: Linda Ruljancich for her grace under pressure, Kathleen Kazinski and Rob Ortman for their encouragement, Brian Templeton for his savvy recommendations, Herman Liebelt for his tireless reviewing and coaching, to the students who asked the difficult questions, and of course, the members of the "Big 10" for sharing their expertise.

Dedicated to those who are pursuing their dreams.

Contents

Introduction

What do Walt Whitman, William Blake, Benjamin Franklin, Gertrude Stein, D.H. Lawrence, James Joyce and Mark Twain all have in common? They once self-published. Throughout history it has been difficult to find a commercial publisher to publish your book, and today it is no different. All is not lost. Self-publishing has become one of the fastest growing segments in the publishing industry and is now more feasible because of the computer. With a computer, desk top software (such as Pagemaker/Ventura/Quark X Press) and a laser printer, anyone can publish a book based on his or her expertise, inspiration or story.

You may have heard success stories of people who self-published and sold tens of thousands of copies. That does happen. However, publishing is a risky business if one is not careful. The fact remains that out of every ten books published, three earn a profit, four break even and the rest lose money. With those kinds of odds it is only sensible to approach this venture wisely. The question remains . . . will *your* book sell?

No one can predict the commercial success of a book. The only way to find out is to give your idea the best possible chance to succeed with the least risk. To write a book is an art, to self-publish one is a business. This is often overlooked until one is stuck with a garage full of unsold books. Your financial risk can be off-set significantly by determining if there is a market for your book. Share your manuscript with people, and ask them for an honest assessment. If you are still enthusiastic, print a small quantity and promote them locally to see if they sell beyond your friends and family. If they sell, print more; if they don't, you are not out a fortune. This is called **test marketing**. Other advantages of testing the water before taking the plunge are making intelligent decisions based on facts, not emotion, keeping your day job until your book proves successful, promoting the book in your free time and learning the best way to sell your book as you find your way around book publishing.

It is **not** the purpose of this book to be a comprehensive guide to book publishing. That is left to others. The **purpose** of this book is to outline the steps in the self-publishing process in a simple and condensed manner. This will answer your initial inquiries: *What do I do first? Whom do I contact?* and *How do I reduce my financial risk?* Studying this book will help you to ask informed questions and to better understand the more comprehensive literature written on this subject. Filled with references, worksheets and money saving ideas, this guide is designed for the cost-conscious self-publisher of a non-fiction book and to a slightly lesser degree a poetry and fiction book.

The book is organized into five chapters: Getting Started, Printing, Announcing Your Book, Distribution and Creating a Demand. Each chapter includes tips and references to guide you through the publishing process. In addition, there are two indexes in the back of the book. Whether you print hundreds or thousands of copies and market them locally or nationally, this book can save you time and money.

Reading this book is a beginning, not an ending. You are urged to add depth to the ideas written on the following pages before you make your final decisions. Self-publishing is not a get-rich-quick scheme and requires hard work and perseverance. I now understand why so many people in this industry have courteously uttered these parting words, similar to those often heard in a gambling casino's token window... **"Good Luck!"**

Mark Ortman
Seattle 1994

Five Reasons to Self-Publish

1.) TIME. Most commercial publishers work on an 18 month production cycle. Do you want to wait that long to get into print? On your own, it can take 4-6 months after completing the manuscript, depending on the complexity of your book.

2.) CONTROL. If you like the final say on the direction of your projects, then self-publishing will give you this freedom. While other people's experience and advice may be beneficial, why give a third party, whose interests and intentions may be different from your own, the final say? Too many cooks can spoil the stew.

3.) MAKE MONEY. Why accept a 5 to 15% royalty when you can have a 40-400% margin or more. Sure a large publisher may have the contacts and will finance the project, but guess who does all the promoting anyway? If your self-published book proves successful, publishers will come knocking on your door. Then you can negotiate from a position of strength.

4.) OWNERSHIP. A commercial publisher would own certain rights to your book, which prevents you from printing copies when he loses interest, allowing him to place your title out of print... unless of course you *purchase* those rights back. A self-publisher may sell all, none or a portion of the rights to the book at any time.

5.) BE IN PRINT. Not everyone publishes to make money. There are several other reasons, such as: seeing your name in print, leaving a legacy to your family or sharing what you have learned with others. Whatever your motive, a book is an expression of you that can open up new possibilities and opportunities. A book takes on a life of its own and you can become a part of that exciting life.

The Three Most Important Questions

Before you decide to publish your own book, know your motivation. Take time to carefully reflect on these three questions, as the answers will help you make some decisions during the publishing process.

1.) WHY is it important to you to publish this book?

2.) WHO will buy your book?

3.) WHY should people read your book?

"The profession of book writing makes horse-racing
seem like a stable business."
John Steinbeck

"If you don't write for publication, there is little point in writing at all."
George Bernard Shaw

1. Getting Started

Learning About the Industry

❑ There are several sources of information to help you learn about the industry. Before you embark on any major project, it only makes sense to familiarize yourself with the lay of the land. Contact the following organizations and publications to request samples and membership information.

American Booksellers Association (ABA)
560 White Plains Road
Tarrytown NY 10591
(800) 637-0037

Also request a list of the regional booksellers associations and a sample of the *American Bookseller* magazine.

COSMET	**PMA**
P.O. Box 703-P	2401 Pacific Coast Hwy #102-A
San Francisco CA 94101	Hermosa Beach CA 90254
(415) 922-9490	(310) 372-2732

These two associations provide co-op membership services to small publishers.

Publishers Weekly	**Small Press Magazine**
P.O. Box 6457	Kymbolde Way
Torrance CA 90504	Wakefield RI 02879
1-800-278-2991	(401) 789-0074

Request a sample copy of the industry's trade journals.

❑ **Visit Local Bookstores.** Tell bookstore managers you are publishing a book and would like to ask questions and get their suggestions. You may want to call in advance to set up a convenient time to meet. After the meeting, send a thank you note. When your book is released they may be more inclined to carry your title, especially if you used their ideas.

❑ **Public Libraries** have a wealth of free information. Visit the reference desk and become familiar with the following publications and any others they recommend for the self-publisher.

Literary Market Place
A valuable resource listing agents, associations, book clubs, reviewers, news services, radio and TV stations.

Books in Print & Forthcoming Books
Lists over 1 million titles currently in print in the United States. Also includes the authors' and publishers' names.

❑ **Read Books.** Benefit from other people's experiences by reading their books on self-publishing. In addition to this book, I find the following publications to be worthwhile and refer to them often. *These books can be ordered directly through the mail by using the order form on page 59.*

⅄ **The Self-Publishing Manual**	**Complete Guide to Self-Publishing**
By Dan Poynter	By Tom & Marilyn Ross
ISBN 0-915516-90-X / $19.95	ISBN 0-89879-354-8 / $18.95

These are two of the most comprehensive books on self-publishing on the market today, including what you need to know to write your own book.

Besides using all the brains we have,
we must use all we can borrow."
Woodrow Wilson

✗ **Book Publishing Resource Guide**
By Marie Kiefer
ISBN 0-912411-38-4 / $25.00

This directory includes the names, addresses, phone numbers, and key contacts for more than 3000 book marketing channels and 5000 publicity outlets.

✗ **1001 Ways to Market Your Book / 4th Edition**
By John Kremer
ISBN 0-912411-42-2 / $19.95

The most complete handbook on book marketing with ideas, tips and suggestions for marketing your own book.

Business Matters

All to often we forget that writing is an art and publishing is a business. For practical, tax and legal reasons it is important to establish a business structure in which your publishing venture can thrive.

❑ Think of a few **names** and **logos** to identify your publishing business. Avoid appearing too small by using your own name. Invent a name that will not limit future publications. Select one that is simple, descriptive and easy to remember. Once you have narrowed your choices, check the following resources in the library for name clearance to avoid duplication with another publisher.

Small Press Record of Books in Print
Directory of US Publishers
Literary Market Place
Books in Print

Tip: Make sure your logo is still legible when reduced to a size that will fit on the spine of a book.

11.

❑ Plan a **budget** for publishing your book. Decisions between what you *want* and what you can *afford* will be easier with a budget. Expect to spend anywhere from $500 to $12,000 depending on the type of book and quantity printed. The three major areas of expense will be:

Book Preparation / Printing / Promotion

> *Tip:* A general guideline for planning the promotional budget is to estimate 25-30% of the cost of your first printing.

❑ Apply for a **Business License** with your state and local governments. Before you apply, decide on a type of business structure: *Sole Proprietorship, Partnership,* or *Corporation.* Most first time publishers choose Sole Proprietorship because it is the easiest to form. Talk to a banker, lawyer or the Small Business Administration for advice on starting a business.

Small Business Administration (SBA)
409 3rd St SW
Washington DC 20416
(800)-827-5722 (Answer Desk)

❑ Rent a **P.O. Box** from the Post Office for a mailing address to protect your privacy. Request information on bulk mailing permits as well as postal rates. Postage will be a major expense, so know your options to reduce mailing costs.

❑ Further professionalize your business image with **Printed Stationery**. Print letterheads, envelopes, business cards and shipping labels with your name, address and logo. You want to project an image which will instill confidence in people who may want to do business with you. Single title author-publishers must overcome the stigma of being perceived as unprofessional.

Trade Registrations

❑ The *International Standard Book Number* **(ISBN)** is the ten digit number on the back of every book. The numbers identify the publisher and book title. The industry uses this number to order, price and keep track of inventory. Most wholesalers and bookstores are reluctant to stock a book that does not have this number clearly printed on the back cover. The numbers are free through R.R. Bowker. However, there is a handling fee of $115. The numbers are available in quantities of 10, 100, or 1000 for the same fee, depending on your needs. They will arrive on a computer printout sheet reserved for your selection. The remaining numbers can be used for your revised editions and future publications.

• After you select a number from the computer printout sheet, register by completing the **Advance Book Information** form **(ABI)** included with your ISBN order. By submitting an ABI form, your book will be listed in *Books in Print* at no charge. Call R.R. Bowker and request a publisher's information package on how to apply for an ISBN number.

R.R. Bowker (ISBN Agency)
121 Chanlon Rd
New Providence NJ 07974
(908) 665-6770

❑ Set a **Publication Date** far enough in the future to give you time to print, submit for review, announce your book and generate advance sales. Your publication date is not the date your book comes back from the printer. The publication date is when you are releasing your book for sale to the public. The two major buying seasons for the publishing industry are January and June. The best publication date for the self-publisher is the first quarter of the year because this allows your copyright date to live a full year and still be new.

❏ **Copyright Protection** lasts your life plus 50 years. This is done by using the copyright symbol with the year and your name (Copyright © 1994 by Mark Ortman) and including it on the copyright page of your manuscript. Also, when your manuscript is complete, send yourself a notarized copy by *registered mail* and place un-opened in storage. This is evidence of a specific date within the copyright year. Finally, when you get your books back from the printer, apply in writing with the copyright office in Washington, DC. *Order in advance the circulars on copywriting and form TX which is package #109. They are free of charge.* Call (202) 707-9100

Registration of Copyrights
Library of Congress
Washington DC 20559

❏ If you plan to make sales to the lucrative library market, apply for a **Library of Congress (LC) Pre-Assigned Card Catalog Number**. Print this number on the copyright page of your book. There is no charge for this number and it can be ordered for any book over 50 pages (with a few exceptions). Request the CIP and PCN publishers manual and forms.

Library of Congress
Cataloging in Publication Division
Washington DC 20540
(202) 707-9797

❏ **Barcodes** (Bookland EAN) are those vertical lines on the back of books. This enables a price scanner at a cash register to identify the title, ISBN number and price. This costs about $30 and you need the ISBN number before you can order one. For more information contact either:

Data Index, Inc.	GGX Associates, Inc.
P.O. Box 500	11 Middle Neck Rd
Kirkland WA 98083	Great Neck NY 11021
(800) 426-2183/(206) 885-9081	(516) 487-6370

Preparing the Manuscript

☐ If you use other people's words (not ideas) in your book, get **permission**. Send a request to the publisher by registered mail stating *what you want to quote, how you will use it* and *where you will give credit in your book.* Normally you will get permission without cost. Remember, copying and selling words of another author without written permission is called plagiarism and is illegal under the law. Consult a copyright Attorney for questions.

☐ **Copy editing.** An editor can clarify and strengthen what you want to say and how you say it. Contact a local newspaper or magazine to see if an editor or writer is willing to moonlight or recommend a colleague. Another option is to find an English teacher or graduate student from a local college or university who would love to receive acknowledgement in your book in exchange for assistance. Get references and samples before you make commitment.

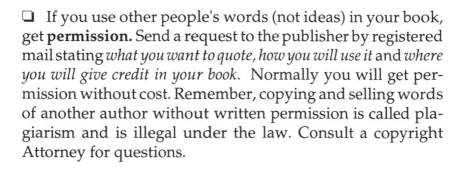

> *Tip:* In copy editing: go slowly, question everything
> and ask yourself, "Are the statements I am
> making true and verifiable?"

☐ Ask five eagle-eyed friends to **proofread** your manuscript for consistency, spelling, usage, punctuation and content. It is not uncommon to rewrite your manuscript a dozen times before it is ready to print . . . so be patient. Changes become costly after the manuscript goes to the printer. Include those people who help in the book's acknowledgments.

> *Tip:* Do not rely on the computer's spell checker since it doesn't
> know whether you want to use "to", "too" or "two".

❑ **Typesetting & Layout.** This has to do with the placement of your illustrations, graphs, pictures and text. In other words, how the inside of your book will look. Research books in bookstores and libraries to use as a model for your own layout. A professional typesetter's fee can range from $6-12 per page. Thus it may be cost-effective to purchase a computer, software and even a printer to do it yourself. Today's laser printers can produce clear camera-ready 300 or 600 DPI output at a reasonable price. The goal of the layout is to make your book easy to read and use. Ask yourself if the text, layout and illustrations all communicate a consistent message throughout your book.

• **Page Layout Margins.** Save money by selecting a standard size for your book: 5.5 x 8.5, 6x9 or 8.5 x 11. The layout margin is the space between the edge of the paper and where the text starts to compensate for trimming during the printing process. Typically a 1/2" to 1" margin is adequate depending on the size of paper and type of binding you use. For example: This book used a 5/8" margin.

• **Typeface & Font.** Most books use a Serif typeface for the *main body* of the text instead of Sans Serif type because it is easier to read and looks more professional. See the sample below. Handwritten copy or calligraphy may be suitable for certain publications, such as poetry or children's books. However, too much handwritten copy is hard to read and may detract from the flavor and intention of your book.

Serif   Sans Serif

• **Illustrations.** Illustrations can range from photographs, artwork, drawings, charts and anything that is not typeset. In planning the layout, leave enough space for the illustrations and either scan them in with a computer or paste them by hand. Consult a graphic artist for the specifics.

The Cover Design

The goal of the cover design is to get people's attention. Books are often sold on the merits of the cover alone; thus the cover should capture the essence of your book. It is worth the investment to hire an experienced **graphic artist**. Expect to pay $100 for a simple one or two color design to over $1000 for a full color camera-ready design.

❑ People's first impressions come from the title of your book. Keep your **book title** brief, vivid and descriptive. The title should be legible from 10 feet so people strolling though the bookstore can read it at a glance. The **subtitle** gives you an added sales message, describing your book in greater detail. Once you have narrowed possible book titles, check *Books in Print* for a title clearance.

❑ If you think the book's **spine** is unimportant in the design, consider how many books in a bookstore are faced out that way. Include on the spine the title of the book, author and publishers name and logo.

❑ The **back cover** should convince the potential book buyers they are making the right decision by purchasing your book. Make it easy, interesting and informative for the browser to review. The back cover might include:

- Book's description and benefits to the reader
- Reviews, Endorsements or Testimonials
- Author's bio and picture
- ISBN, Bar Code, Price and Subject Catagory

❑ The easiest way to get **testimonials** or **endorsements** is to ask for them. Ask experts or celebrities in your field to review your manuscript and submit their impressions. Get permission in writing to print their comments on your book cover.

"Whenever I am asked what kind of writing is the most lucrative . . . I have to say, ransom notes!"

H. N. Swanson

2. Printing

Book Manufacturers

Get bids from a *Book Manufacturer* instead of a local printer. Book manufacturers have the equipment to print and bind books themselves, instead of sending out the work and marking up the price. If your book is more than 60 pages and you are printing over 500 copies, chances are the prices will be more competitive through a book manufacturer.

❑ Cheapest isn't always best. Consider **quality, service,** and **support.** If a problem arises, and printing is fertile ground for problems, whose side will your printer be on, yours or his? Paying a little more for peace of mind is often worth it. Request samples, and check references before you decide.

❑ Order **Blueline Proofs** before your book goes to press. This means you'll see and approve what the book will look like before it is printed. Check for typographical errors or pages missing or out of sequence. There may be a charge for this service, but it is comforting to have the chance to make last minute changes. Make copies of the blueline to use as a **galley** as some reviewers require your book in this form.

❑ Most printers will print about 10% too many or too few books. These are called **over-** or **under-runs.** Ask what the over-runs will cost. They usually cost less, thus lowering the overall cost per copy of your book. Reprints are usually less expensive from the same printer because of reduced setup costs. Still, get other quotes to keep everyone honest.

❏ It's more economical to print in **Even Signatures.** This means the number of pages a printing press can print at one time. Most book manufacturers use a 16 or 32 page signature. Divide the pages of your book into 16 or 32 and you will know how many signatures the printer will use. If your book is a page or two over an even signature, reduce the printing cost by editing out a page or two.

❏ **The Retail Price.** Search bookstores for comparable books to use as a price model. A common mistake for self-publishers is to price their book either too high or too low. Find the right price. Printing costs do affect the retail price of the book, but don't expect your first printing to be extremely profitable, particularly when printing a small quantity. Reprints are more profitable because of reduced printing costs assuming you don't make many changes to the book. Keep in mind the percentage you will give away for distribution *(See page 35).*

Preparing a Printing Estimate

To prepare a price quote from a book manufacturer, you will need to know:

- Quantity
- Total page count
- Type of paper (text & cover)
- How many colors on the cover (cover coating?)
- Type of binding
- Size of the book
- Number of halftones for pictures
- Packaging and shipping costs

❏ **Quantity.** How many books should you order? The more you print, the less each costs. Strike a balance between printing enough copies to keep your unit cost down and too many copies where you're stuck with a garage full of unsold books. Typically, small publishers will order between 500 and 3500 books in the first printing. The only time to order more is if most are pre-sold. You can always re-order when your inventory gets low. Reprints generally cost less if there are not many changes made (changes require the cost of new printing plates to be made). Plan on 4 to 6 weeks for delivery.

❏ **Page Count.** To figure the total page count in your book, include the *front* and *the back* matter. The front matter is all the pages before the main text such as: Title Pages, Copyright Page, Acknowledgments, Preface, Foreword, Introduction, Table of Contents, Dedication. The back matter includes all pages in a book after the main text: Afterword, Appendix, Bibliography, Glossary, Index, etc...

❏ **Paper.** Unless you are doing an art or specialty book, most printers will suggest a 50, 60, or 70lb white offset. (Recycled paper is more expensive.) The higher the weight, the heavier and less opaque the paper. The thickness (bulk) of the paper is measured by PPI (Pages per inch). Ask the printer for this number to determine the width of the book's spine. The lower the PPI, the bulkier the paper, thus the thicker the book.

> *Tip:* One of your greatest expenses will be postage and shipping. The paper you select will influence this expense. Heavier paper costs more to ship.

❏ **Cover Paper.** Softcover or hardcover? Because of production costs, most books are now softcover. The standard paper for softcover is a 10 or 12 point C1S (coated one side) cover stock. Hardcover books will use a sleeve, and 80 lb enamel paper is most common. As they are being printed with your book, order a few hundred extra covers and take advantage of the reduced over-run price. They can be used later for numerous book promotions.

❑ **Cover Coating.** This is what protects the book cover and enhances the color. There are various kinds available, such as plastic lamination, UV, varnish or aqueous coating. Ask the printers what type they use, the advantages of each, and to send you samples.

❑ **Binding.** This is what holds the book together. The four general types are: Perfect Bound (softcover), Case Bound (hardcover), Spiral, or Saddle Stitched (stapled). How the book will be used will influence the type of binding. The most popular and prudent is Perfect Bound.

> *Tip:* Bookstores frown upon Spiral and Saddle Stitched because you can't read them when faced spine out on the shelf.

❑ **Book Size.** The conventional and common 5.5x8.5 is suitable for both hardcover and soft, and is the most economical to print. Other standard sizes include 6x9 and 8.5x11. The further you get away from the standard, the more expensive it is to produce.

❑ **Pictures.** Color photos can be beautiful, although the cost may be prohibitive because of color separation and extra print run fees. B&W photos are more practical and affordable. All B&W photographs require halftones. The process of creating a halftone converts the picture into dots of various sizes and shades of gray. The more dots per inch, the clearer the picture. Most halftones for books are produced at 120-133 dots per inch. Consult your graphic artist for details.

❑ **Packaging.** Ask your printer how to economically ship your books, and the size and weight of the cartons to plan for storage. A packaging option to consider is shrink wrapping. This is a clear plastic wrap used to protect the books and should be considered if you intend to store your books in a garage or unheated storage area.

List of Book Manufacturers

These printers specialize in the manufacturing of books. For additional listings, see the *Literary Market Place* in a library. Get all estimates **in writing** before you make a decision.

BookCrafters
613 E. Industrial Dr
Chelsea MI 48118
(313) 475-9145
Fax (313) 475-7337

McNaughton & Gunn
960 Woodland Dr
Saline MI 48176
(313) 429-5411
Fax (313) 429-4033

Patterson Printing
155 Territorial Rd
Benton Harbor MI 49022
(616) 925-2177
Fax (616) 925-6057

Malloy Lithographing
5411 Jackson Rd
Ann Arbor MI 48106
(313) 655-6113
Fax (313) 665-2326

Edwards Brothers
2500-P South State St
Ann Arbor MI 48104
(313) 769-1000
Fax (313) 769-0350

Gilliland Printing
215 North Summit
Arkansas City KS 67005
(316) 442-8500
Fax (316) 442-8504

Rose Printing
P.O. Box 5078
Tallahassee FL 32314
(904) 576-4151
Fax (905) 576-4153

Publishers Press
1900 West 2300 South
Salt Lake City UT 84119
(801) 972-6600
Fax (801) 972-6601

Thomson-Shore
7300 West Joy Rd
Dexter MI 48130
(313) 426-3939
Fax (313) 426-6219

Data Reproductions
1480 N. Rochester Rd
Rochester Hills MI 48207
(313) 652-7600
Fax (313) 652-7605

Printing Estimate Worksheet

Printer: _____

Book Title: _____

Quantity: _____ Trim Size: _____ x _____ Pages: _____

Photos/Halftones: _____   ❏ Color   ❏ B & W   ❏ Bleeds

Paper

    ❏ 50 Lb Book   ❏ Other: _____

    ❏ 60 Lb Book   ❏ Color: _____

Cover

    ❏ 10 pt. C1S   ❏ 80 Lb Enamal (Hardcover)

    ❏ 12 Pt. C1S   ❏ Other: _____

Cover Colors / Coating

Cover color Black + _____ PMS Colors

Bleeds?   Yes   No

Cover Coating: _____

Quantity of extra covers: _____

Binding

❏ Perfect (Soft)   ❏ Case (Hard)   ❏ Spiral   ❏ Staple (Saddle)

Copy & Cover to be furnished:

❏ Text camera-ready   ❏ Cover Negatives   ❏ Computer Disk

Cost per book of over-runs: _____

Cost per extra 1000 books ordered: _____

Shipping Costs & Instructions:

Printing Estimate Worksheet

Printer: _____ _____

Book Title: _____

Quantity: _____ Trim Size: _____ x _____ Pages: _____

Photos/Halftones: _____   ❑ Color   ❑ B & W   ❑ Bleeds

Paper

    ❑ 50 Lb Book   ❑ Other: _____

    ❑ 60 Lb Book   ❑ Color: _____

Cover

    ❑ 10 pt. C1S   ❑ 80 Lb Enamal (Hardcover)

    ❑ 12 Pt. C1S   ❑ Other: _____

Cover Colors / Coating

Cover color Black + _____ PMS Colors

Bleeds?   Yes   No

Cover Coating: _____

Quantity of extra covers: _____

Binding

❑ Perfect (Soft)   ❑ Case (Hard)   ❑ Spiral   ❑ Staple (Saddle)

Copy & Cover to be furnished:

❑ Text camera-ready   ❑ Cover Negatives   ❑ Computer Disk

Cost per book of over-runs: _____

Cost per extra 1000 books ordered: _____

Shipping Costs & Instructions:

"There are books of which the backs and covers are by far the best parts."

Charles Dickens

3. Announcing Your Book

Letting the Industry Know

❏ Let the book trade know you have published a book. Orders can come most unexpectedly by having your title listed in several directories. Most of these listings are free. Write or phone to request an application.

International Standard Book Numbering Agency (ISBN)
When you submit your **ABI** (Advanced Book Information) form with your publication date and ISBN number, you will automatically be listed in *Books in Print*.

Library of Congress Catalog Card Number.
When you request an LC number, your book will be listed in a catalog enabling libraries to locate your book more easily.

Cumulative Book Index & Vertical File Index
H.W. Wilson Co
950 University Avenue
Bronx NY 10452
(718) 588-8400

Small Press Record of Books in Print & International Directory of Little Magazines and Small Presses.
Dustbooks
P.O. Box 100-P
Paradise CA 95967
(916) 877-6110

Book Publishers in the United States and Canada.
Gale Research
835 Penobscot Bldg.
Detroit MI 48226
(313) 961-2242

Pre-Publication Reviews

In addition to yourself, who else thinks your book is great? Pre-publication reviews are directed at the trade (libraries, wholesalers and bookstores) before the publication date and the release of your book. This helps the trade evaluate new titles and influences its purchasing decisions.

❑ **Trade Reviews.** At least 90 days *before* your publication date, send to the major review magazines listed below,galleys (NOT a book), a photocopy of your ABI form, sample of the cover art (if possible), and a cover letter describing *why* you wrote the book and *how* it can be used. Send by first class mail. There is no guarantee your book will be reviewed. However, one favorable review could generate substantial advance sales. In addition, any reviews you receive can be used on your promotional literature and printed on the back cover of reprinted books. It is worth a phone call to inquire about the full name (with correct spelling) of the appropriate person to whom to submit a review package. See *Literary Market Place* for a list of more reviewers.

Booklist
American Library Association
50 East Huron St
Chicago IL 60611
(312) 944-6780

Chicago Tribune Books
435 N Michigan Ave
Chicago Il 60611
(312) 222-3232

Kirkus Reviews
200 Park Avenue South
New York NY 10003
(212) 777-4554

Library Journal
249 West 17th St
New York NY 10011
(212) 645-0067

L.A. Times Book Review	N.Y. Times Review of Books
Times Mirror Square	250 West 57th St
Los Angeles CA 90053	New York NY 10107
(213) 237-5000	(212) 757-8070

The N.Y. Times Book Review	Publishers Weekly
229 West 43rd St, 8th Fl.	249 West 17th St
New York NY 10036	New York NY 10011
(212) 556-1942	(212) 645-0067

San Francisco Chronicle Book Review	Small Press
275 Fifth St	Kymbolde Way
San Francisco CA 94103	Wakefield RI 02879
(415) 777-7042	(401) 789-0074

San Francisco Review of Books	The Washington Post
2909 McClure St	1150 15th St N.W.
Oakland CA 94609	Washington DC 10071
(415) 252-7708	(202) 334-7882

• **Galleys.** A galley is not a finished book, but a representation of the finished book. Instead of paying to have galleys printed and bound, consider making copies of the blueline proofs you received from the printer. This means printing your book over three months before the publication date. Another option is to send a photocopy of your camera-ready manuscript.

• **News Release.** The best news releases are those which read like a well written newspaper article. On one page answer: *Who, What, Why, When* and *Where* . . . not in a self-serving manner, but factually. Stay away from hype, and focus on what problem your book solves and its value. At the end of the article, include the specifics such as publication date, number of pages, price, ISBN number and even a small B&W photo and halftone of the book cover.

Post-Publication Reviews

Post-publication reviews are intended to reach the purchaser of your book. It is very expensive and inefficient to send review copies to every book reviewer. Target those from whom you have the best chance of getting a review.

❏ **Newspaper Reviewers.** Most newspaper book reviewers receive more solicitations daily than they can review in a month. Review space is at a premium. Nevertheless, any mention of your book will help sales. At least 45 days before your release date, mail a news release and book request return postcard to the more than 500 major newspapers in the country. Rent a mailing list from one of the mailing list brokers on page 51. Community newspapers and magazines are your best bets to get a book review or an article. Because you are local news, they will be more inclined to give you preference over others.

❏ **Magazine Reviews.** Target those who will purchase and read your book. Find out what magazines *they* read and send a copy of your book, a press release and cover letter to those magazines' book review editors. See the *Book Publishing Resource Guide* by *Marie Kiefer,* or a copy of *Magazines for Libraries* in the public library for listings of specialty magazines.

❏ **Free-Lance Reviewers.** Rent a mailing list of free-lance book reviewers around the country (see page 51). Send a news release, copy of your ABI form, and a book request return postcard 45 days before the book is released.

❏ **Experts in the Field.** Send a review copy to authorities or experts on the subject of your book asking for their endoresements. This is a wonderful way to get influential people talking about your book. See *Who's Who in America* at the local library for their names and addresses.

❏ **Newsletter Reviews.** The number of newsletters now published has boomed during the past decade. This has resulted in more opportunities to get your book reviewed or mentioned for your market audience to see. See the *Oxbridge Directory of Newsletters* in the local library.

• **Review Copies.** Giving books away can become an expensive proposition, particularly when you include the cost of postage. A simple rule is to budget *at least* 10% of the books from your first printing as review copies and give them to the people who can *do you the most good*. Be flexible in giving away review copies as they can be an extremely good investment. Of course, with your second printing, you can afford to be more liberal in your giveaways. Stamp REVIEW COPY, NOT FOR SALE on any copy you give away to discourage people from selling or returning that book to wholesalers for a refund. Keep good records of giveaways as they are a tax-deductible business expense.

Book Review Tips

Choose only those reviewers most
suitable to the subject of your book.

Follow up immediately with anyone who
requests a review copy of your book.

Don't be suprised if you don't get an
overwhelming response from all the reviewers.

"Publishing is a very mysterious business. It is hard to predict what kind of sale or reception a book will have."
Thomas Wolfe

*"Literature is like any other trade;
you will never sell anything unless
you go to the right shop."*

George Bernard Shaw

4. Distribution

Distribution Channels

How are people going to find your book if they decide to buy it? Reviews, publicity and promotion are worthless unless your book is easily available to the buyer. At least two months before the release date, decide on how you will distribute your book, whether through conventional, alternative or a combination of both channels of distribution.

❑ **Consignments.** This means you don't get paid until after your book is sold. This is a standard practice in the publishing industry, especially in the conventional channels of distribution. All books are sold on a consignment basis unless terms are negotiated differently. Also, it is common practice to return all unsold books to you when the demand ceases.

❑ **Marketing Plan.** Most channels of distribution want to know how *you* are going to create a demand for your book if they stock it. That's right, the self-publisher is responsible for creating the demand. Before you approach the conventional channels of distribution, have a 12 month step-by-step marketing plan which answers:

* **WHO** will buy your book?
* **WHY** will they buy your book?
* **HOW** will they know about your book?
* **WHAT** are you going to do to create a demand?
* **WHEN** will each step of the plan be implemented?

Conventional Channels of Distribution

❏ **Bookstores.** There are many kinds of bookstores: General, Used, College, Religious to list a few. Independently owned bookstores make up nearly half of all the bookstores in the United States. Half of those (and growing) are chains such as Barnes & Noble, B. Dalton, Waldenbooks and Crown. The standard bookstore discount is 40 to 43% off the list price and they purchase a majority of their books through wholesalers. Most bookstores prefer buying books through a wholesaler or distributor because they carry numerous titles, simplifying their ordering procedure. *The American Book Trade Directory* in the library has bookstore listings.

❏ **Chain Bookstores.** Growing segments in the industry are the chains and superstores. Their inventories are tightly controlled with short shelf life for slow-moving books. Recognize the risk of selling to the chains. They may order your entire stock and pay you 90 days later, leaving you to finance the next printing. Then, all of a sudden, they return the unsold books asking for a refund. A more cautious approach would be to coordinate purchases and promotional effort with local or regional chain buyers. This way the sales of one area finance the expansion into another. Why risk putting all your books in one basket?

❏ **Wholesalers.** Wholesalers stock, pick, pack, ship and collect, then pay you 90 days later on orders received for your book. For this service, they want a 55% discount off the list price. Most are *"Demand Wholesalers"* meaning they fulfill orders for your book based on the demand that *you* create. There are hundreds of book wholesalers in the country, some national, some regional and many specializing in niche markets. To find their specialties, consult the *Book Publishing Resource Guide* by *Marie Kiefer* or *Literary Market Place* in the library.

INGRAM Book Company and **Baker & Taylor Books** are the nation's largest general book wholesalers with branches throughout the United States. Contact each of them and ask how to start a vendor account.

Baker & Taylor Books	INGRAM Book Company
652 East Main St	1125 Heil Quaker Blvd
Bridgewater NJ 08807	LaVergne TN 37086
(908) 218-3803	(615) 793-5000 Ext 7584

Is your book of mainly local or regional interest? Ask local booksellers which regional wholesaler(s) they order through. Contact that wholesaler, tell him your marketing plans, and establish a vendor account.

❏ **Distributors.** Distributors differ from wholesalers in that they sell your book through commissioned sales reps and a catalog. Depending on your marketing plan and the nature of your book, a distributor will introduce your title to wholesalers and bookstores, thus freeing you to concentrate on promotion. Their fee is 55% to 70% off the list price. Some may require an exclusive arrangement. Before signing an exclusive agreement, clarify **what** is meant by "exclusive". Do not limit your book to an exclusive arrangement, preventing you from selling to markets which the distributor doesn't sell to. Contact distributors at least 60 days before your book is released to allow enough time to go through their selection committees. Listed next are the various types of distributors. See the *Literary Market Place* or the *Book Publishing Resource Guide* for additional listings.

• **Mass Market Distributors.** If your book fits their format they will place your title in non-bookstore locations such as supermarkets, airports, and newsstands. Their fee: 55% off list. Require all returns in resaleable condition. Mass Market distributors traditionally have a high return rate and a short shelf life. If a book doesn't sell fast, it is replaced.

• **Specialty Distributors.** When your book is targeted toward a specific niche or subject area (Outdoor, Health, Ethnic, etc.), specialty distributors can help you reach that reader. Their fees vary between 55% to 70% off list.

• **Library Distributors.** They specialize in selling books to libraries. Contact the two distributors listed below and ask for a vendor application. Both want a 55% discount and pay 90 days after each book is sold.

Quality Books	**Unique Books**
918 Sherwood Dr	4230 Grove Ave
Lake Bluff IL 60044	Gurnee IL 60031
(708) 259-2010	(708) 623-9171

• **National General Distributors.** If your book is of general interest and you plan to promote your title nationally, contract a general titled national distributor to carry your book. A distributor will get your book into the major regional and national book wholesalers and perhaps present your title to major independant and chain bookstores. A distributor will coordinate your promotional efforts with his national sales rep network. Distributors want a 65-70% discount off list. Below are six national distributors you can request information from on their title acquisition procedure. Most will want an exclusive right to sell in the book trade (bookstores and libraries). That leaves you to sell through alternative channels. Have a detailed marketing plan before approaching these distributors.

BookWorld Services, Inc.	**Independent Publishers Group**
1933 Whitfield Loop	814 North Franklin St
Sarasota FL 34243	Chicago IL 60610
(813) 758-8094	(312) 337-0747

Login Publishers Consortium
1436 W. Randolph St
Chicago IL 60607
(312) 733-8228

National Book Network
4720 Boston Way
Lanham MD 20706
(301) 459-8696

Publishers Distribution Service
6893 Sullivan Rd
Grawn MI 49637
(616) 276-5196

Publishers Group West
4065 Hollis St
Emeryville CA 94608
(510) 658-3453

Alternative Channels of Distribution

If your book does not have broad, general appeal for conventional channels of distribution, all is not lost. Most books sold in the United States are sold through alternative channels. Books on a specific subject or niche may find alternative channels easiest to secure and most profitable. Consult the *Literary Market Place* or *The Book Publishing Resource Guide* for additional listings of alternative distributors.

❑ **Book Clubs.** Book clubs may be interested in purchasing book club rights or actual copies of your book when printed. While some special interest book clubs will buy books regardless of the publication date, most prefer at least 6 months notice before the publication date.

❑ **Catalog Houses.** Have you ever received a catalog in the mail that featured books? Thousands of companies in the United States send out catalogs annually, many including books. Send a copy of your book before the publication date to mail order catalog companies that specialize in the subject area of your title. For mail order catalogs that feature books see *Directory of Mail Order Catalogs* by Grey House Publishing at the public library.

❑ **Gift Representatives.** Over 30% of the population have never been in a bookstore. Having your book displayed in retail outlets such as gift and card shops is a way to reach some of those people. Unlike bookstores, the gift market does not return books. However, the discount is a little higher; generally 50% off list. Gift representatives present your title to buyers at a 10-15% commission. You are then responsible for shipping and invoicing the books they sell.

❑ **Special Sales.** Home improvement centers, drugstores, auto supply dealers, kitchen shops, health-food stores are all prospects if your book fits their niche. In other words, approach people or companies who can tie your book into the marketing of their own products. Most of these sales are made on a non-return basis.

❑ **Direct Sales.** Any sales made bypassing a middle man are your most profitable. You keep 100% of the retail price less any expenses and negotiated discounts.

❑ **Fulfillment Services.** These companies offer warehousing and order-processing services (1-800 numbers & credit card purchases over the phone) for your book. Most want a 40% to 50% discount off list. As you promote your title, make reference to the service's 1-800 number for ordering 24 hours a day. Shipping and handling costs are paid for by the purchaser. Contact the following about their services:

Twin Peaks Press
P.O. Box 129
Vancouver WA 98666
(206) 694-2462

Upper Access
P.O. Box 457
Hinesburg VT 05461
(802) 482-2988

Publishers Distribution Service
6893 Sullivan Rd
Grawn MI 49637
(616) 276-5196

BookMasters, Inc.
638 Jefferson St
Ashland OH 44805
(419) 289-6051

❏ **Subsidiary Rights.** This is when you sell the rights of all or a portion of your book to someone else who will package it in a different form for his market. Examples include movie rights, TV rights, an excerpt for a magazine article, paperback version of a hardcover and foreign rights to overseas markets, to list a few.

❏ **Remainder Dealers.** Remainder dealers help liquidate overstocks and remaining copies of your out-of-print books. They will purchase unsold books at pennies on the dollar. When all sales sources are exhausted, contact several remainder dealers to see who will give you the best price and terms.

❏ **Donations.** Another way to liquidate unsold books is to simply donate remaining and damaged books to a worthy cause or non-profit groups and take the tax write-off.

❏ **Discount Schedule/Policy.** Set a discount policy from the very start that is simple, clear and in writing so there is no misunderstanding. It is a requirement by the FTC that any discount you offer one dealer must be given to others who buy the same quantity. Your terms may differ when dealing with conventional channels of distribution as they typically work on a consignment basis only. Include in your Terms and Conditions statement:

- Who pays the shipping and from where
- Breakdown of the quantity discount schedule
- Payment terms
- How to establish credit with you
- Return policy (if any)
- Special services such as *dropshipping*

"Writing is the only profession where no one considers you ridiculous if you earn no money."
Jules Renard

"The writing of a bestseller represents only a fraction of the total effort required to create one."

Ted Nicholas

5. Creating a Demand

Developing a Marketing Plan

Marketing your book is generally the most important and demanding aspect of self-publishing. There are over 500 new titles released each week, over one million books in print and the average bookstore stocks only 25,000 titles. This contributes to a very crowded and competitive environment. The trade has just one question: **"Will your book sell?"**

A book is a product, and like any other product requires publicity and promotion. Potential buyers must be made **aware** of your book and **how** it differs from similar books on the market and **where** they can purchase it. Proper planning is essential to give your book the best chance of success; in other words. . . develop a marketing plan. When you know where you are going, it is easier to get there.

❏   A Marketing Plan answers the questions: *WHO* will buy your book, *HOW* will you reach those people, and *WHEN* will you reach those people?

• **WHO?** A technique to help you figure out *Who will buy your book* is to brainstorm a list of organizations, occupations, associations, hobbyists and anyone who will find value in owning your book. List those you want to reach first, second, third, etc. Review the list and see if there is any overlap. This will help you direct your efforts most efficiently and give you insight into HOW to best reach your customer.

• **HOW?** How will you let the reader know about your book and where to purchase copies? The self-publisher actually has two catagories of customers: *The Trade* and *The Consumer.* The Trade consists of bookstores, wholesalers and libraries. The consumer is your audience. Marketing efforts should be allocated to both. There are five ways to reach people through your promotions: *Mail, Fax, Phone, Media* and *In Person,* each having its advantages and disadvantages. Your choice of distribution may help determine the medium by which you will reach your audience. People today are more accessible, yet harder to sell, stressing the importance of a strong sales message.

Tip: It is not uncommon for a talk show host to receive over 50 solicitations for interviews or publicity each week. In such a crowded arena, a weak message will get little response. Telephone is the most effective way to reach these people.

• **WHEN.** When is the Trade and the Consumer in the most favorable buying mood? Does your book have a seasonal twist? Publishers introduce new releases throughout the year with an emphasis on two seasons: January and June. The industry's largest trade show, the American Bookseller Association convention, occurs annually on the last weekend of May. This is a key time for publishers to show their new titles to the Trade. Consumers purchase books throughout the year with an emphasis on the holiday and gift seasons. The nature of your book is also a consideration as the timing may be built into your product and the reader or industry you intend to reach.

"I have no fans. You know what I got? Customers!
Mickey Spillane

Promotional Tool Kit

There is no limit to what you can spend on promotional materials. It becomes a question of budget and what is practical. Below are suggestions for a basic promotional tool kit for the budget minded self-publisher.

• **News Release.** The one page news release answers *Who, What, When, Where,* and *Why* concentrating on what problem your book will solve for the reader. This is what is mailed to announce the release of your book to reviewers, bookstores and the media. Keep it simple, informative, interesting and factual.

• **Extra Book Covers.** Extra book covers come in handy as mailers, point of purchase display or can be used as part of your media kit. Many distributors will request extra covers for their sales force to use to sell your title.

• **Media Kit.** This is sent to the media to prepare them for an interview. Include background about the author, details about the book and a list of possible interview questions. Make it informative and straightforward as most interviewers will not read your book.

• **Photos.** Order black and white promo glossies of the front cover of your book and another one of you. Pictures are sometimes requested by reviewers, magazines, newspapers and bookstores to promote signings. Include them in some of your mailings in the hope of a picture beside a review or article. The following company specializes in quantity discounted glossies.

Ornaal Glossies, Inc.
24 West 25th St
New York NY 10010
(800) 826-6312

• **Reviews & Endorsements & Letters.** Save any reviews, endorsements, testimonials, fan mail and articles written about you or your book. These provide great sales copy for your promotional literature.

• **ABI Form.** Include a completed Advance Book Information form in your mailings to all pre-publication reviewers. This gives them pertinent book information, and is helpful to qualify and write a review.

• **Book Request Postcards.** Print book request return postcards and include one with your press release when you are not sending a review copy of your book. Those interested in your press release message will respond, thus saving you the expense of mailing books randomly to uninterested people.

• **Brochure or Flyer.** A full color flyer is useful, catchy and professional. A helpful hint is to leave some blank space on the front or the back side to photocopy a specific promotional message at a future date. This enables you to adjust your flyer's message and use for many promotional situations. Shop around, as prices vary from printer to printer.

• **Specialty Advertising.** If your budget permits, imprinted bookmarks, pens, T-shirts, buttons, coffee mugs and the like are a fun giveaway and reminder of your book. It is not uncommon to charge people for unique or unusual specialty advertising items and they can become a part of your product line.

"Success comes to a writer, as a rule, so gradually
that it is something of a shock to him to look back
and realize the heights to which he has climbed."
P.G. Wodehouse

Ways to Create a Demand

The most consuming facet of self-publishing is to create a demand for your book. Few titles come off the press instant best-sellers. Listed below are some of the more popular ways to make people aware of your book. With so many options, self-publishers have the luxury of time to systematically test several promotional stategies to find what works best. What works for one book may not work for another. A more comprehensive collection of ideas can be found in *1001 Ways to Market Your Book* by *John Kremer.*

❑ **Book Signings.** Unless your signing is backed by a great deal of media promotion it is doubtful that people will be lined up waiting for your autograph. However, the signing serves other purposes: it gets your book displayed in the store, you begin building a relationship with the store owner, manager and staff; they become familiar with your title and may recommend it to their customers; and you leave behind signed copies which increase the book's appeal. Most book-stores are receptive to signings, as your presence will help pull customers into their store, resulting in free publicity for them. Send the local media advance notice of your signing; most will list this free.

❑ **More on Libraries.** There are over 100,000 libraries in the United States ranging from Academic to Public Libraries, and they buy a lot of books. Libraries will purchase your book at the profitable list price and your title becomes a permanent advertisement when sitting on their shelf. Do not overlook local libraries for generating publicity and reviews through signings, workshops and lectures. Many Public libraries have an events coordinator or "Friends of the Library" groups who organize author and fundraising activities.

"Nothing happens until something is sold."

❏ **Readings & Lectures**. Local social, civic and business organizations are all looking for speakers. Use your expertise and promote your book. Most groups will let you sell directly to members after the presentation.

❏ **Seminars.** If you enjoy teaching and speaking, find a group, business or organization to sponsor and promote your seminar. This will help offset any costs incurred and provide a built-in endorsement for your book.

❏ **Write an Article.** Since you know more about your topic than most people, share your knowledge and promote your book at the same time. There are many newsletters, magazines, journals and newspapers that welcome newsworthy articles.

❏ **Trade Shows & Conventions.** Selling your book at a trade show or convention can be a profitable experience. Assembled in one place is a high concentration of potential buyers. This becomes a great place to make valuable contacts and get exposure to an industry. Use the *Encyclopedia of Associations* in the library to find out what groups are holding meetings or conventions in your vicinity. The *Chamber of Commerce* and the city's *Convention Centers* are also helpful.

❏ **Book Trade Shows**. The primary purpose of a regional or national book trade show is to introduce new titles to the trade. You may display your new book on your own or pay someone else to do so. Bookstore owners who attend will browse and make seasonal buying decisions; this is an ideal opportunity to win shelf space in their stores.

❏ **Book, Art & Street Fairs.** Sponsors promote to the general public or to a niche group of people and thus are a great forum for showing and selling your book direct. Calculate your break-even point before paying for space. Collaborating with another author is one way to reduce costs.

❏ **Fundraisers.** Most groups, schools and organizations are looking for ways to generate revenues. If there is a subject tie-in, donate a percentage of your book sales to their cause in exchange for selling and endorsing your book.

❏ **Premium & Incentive.** Many businesses offer premiums as incentives to their employees and customers. Why shouldn't that premium be your book? See the *Thomas Registry* in the library for a listing of companies and products to find a tie-in.

❏ **Book Awards & Contests.** An award or even being nominated for a book award can be a profitable and satisfying experience. Submit your title to the various organizations who offer such contests. See the *Literary Market Place* or *Writer's Market* in the library for a listing.

❏ **The Media.** The media (radio, newspapers, television and magazines) is under pressure to fill space or time with news. Make you and your book sound newsworthy and interesting before approaching them. The media is a great way to get free publicity. Locally, you and your book are news and should have an edge to get air time or print space. See *The Directory of Publications and Broadcast Media* in the library. In addition to mail list brokers, the following companies sell ways to reach the national media.

Radio-TV Interview Report	Talk Show Selects
Bradley Communications Corp.	Broadcast Interview Source
135 E Plumstead Ave	2233 Wisconsin Ave NW
Lansdowne PA 19050	Washington DC 20007
(215) 259-1070	(202) 333-4904
(800) 989-1400	(800) 955-0311

"The oldest books are still only just out
to those who have not read them."
Samuel Butler

- **Radio.** If you enjoy talking about your book, then you will enjoy radio interviews. There are over 750 radio talk shows in the country looking for interesting guests. Many conduct interviews over the phone, which means you don't have to leave your home. Some will even tape an interview to be aired at a future date. Phone the Program Director or Producer of the station and ask if they do author interviews. Be prepared to explain why your message will be important to their listeners. Make having an interview with you sound appealing. Start off by interviewing on smaller stations to practice your message for the larger ones.

Assume the interviewer has not read your book. This is the case more often than not and he will rely on the materials you send him in advance. Your *Media Kit* should include detailed information about the author, about the book, and possible interview questions the interviewer could ask. Radio is one of the most accessible forms of publicity. (Phone bookstores prior to your radio interview to insure they have your book in stock. See *The American Book Trade Directory* in the library.)

- **Newspapers.** Perhaps your book solves a lifestyle, business, gardening, travel or cooking problem. Direct an article you have written to the appropriate editor, with permission to use all or part of your writing. If your book solves a problem that just hit the headlines, get on the phone and try to secure an interview. There are over 700 daily and weekly newspapers throughout the country searching for news.

- **Magazines.** There are thousands of magazines catering to every market niche you can imagine. Offer re-prints of a portion of your book in exchange for a free ad and/or a by-line at the end of your article. Do not neglect local and regional publications as they may be more accomodating to local authors. See *Magazines for Libraries* at the public library for a compete listing of magazines and their focus.

• **Television.** Wouldn't it be nice to have some of the major national talk show hosts invite you on their shows to discuss your book? That exposure would translate into an explosion of book sales. More realistic is being a guest on a local afternoon news program or a TV magazine talk show. Contact the show's producer with your story convincing him or her of a possible story angle for the show. TV leaves a memorable impression in the viewer's mind and can translate into short and long term book sales.

> *Tip:* If you are promoting your title through conventional channels of distribution, **inform** your wholesaler, distributor and bookstores of your promotional activities. This will insure they have your book on hand to fufill the demand you create, thus not losing sales.

❏ **Word-of-mouth Advertising.** The fastest and most efficient form of free publicity is word-of-mouth advertising. Anything you can do to get people talking about your book will result in book sales. Publicity, promotion, favorable reviews and advertising all contribute to word-of-mouth advertising. The more books in people's hands, the better the chance they will spread the word. Success begets success.

❏ **Advertising.** Avoid paying for advertising until you have exhausted all forms of free publicity. Advertising comes in many forms, although the intent is always the same: to motivate people to buy. This is done by developing an ad that gains the reader's favorable attention, holds it long enough to get the intended message across and then motivates a desired response. When designing an ad, talk about the readers' interest, as they are interested in **gaining, saving, doing** or **being** something. Two rules of advertising success are **Timing** and **Repetition.**

- **Space Advertising:** Space advertising involves placing an ad in books, newspapers, catalogs and magazines to reach your target audience. Orders are placed by the customer and received by you or your fulfillment service by mail or telephone (800 number) and shipped via the mail. At the reference desk in the public library see:

Standard Rate and Data
Lists magazines, periodicals, demographics and their advertising rates.

Magazines for Libraries
Directory of national magazines by R.R. Bowker

Directory of Publications & Broadcast Media
Listing daily and weekly newspapers in the United States.

- **Classified Ads.** This is one of the least expensive forms of advertising. Classified ads are not used to sell something so much as to compile a good mailing list. The objective is to pull in inquiries about your book. A mailing list compiled from classified responses should yield high order levels. Offer free information in the ad by requesting a self-addressed, stamped envelope (SASE). Then send an article, flyer, brochure or any other promotional material. Code your ads to keep track of what works and what doesn't.

Tip: Before making a sizable investment in advertising, start small to test the effectiveness of your message. This way you can adjust your message until it yields the best results.

"Half the money I spend on advertising is a waste; the trouble is, I don't know which half."
John Wanamaker

- **Direct Mail Response Advertising.** If you can accurately identify your audience or niche, it is possible to sell books by direct mail from your home. Ask yourself: Am I prepared to handle the incoming mail response or should I use a fulfillment service? Is my product suitable to direct mail? Where can I advertise? Associations generally sell membership mailing lists or contact a mailing list broker. See *Encyclopedia of Associations* in the library for a listing of national associations.

Check into the legal regulations of mail order advertising in your state to follow the guidelines set forth by law. Write to the FTC and phone your State's Attorney General's office and request information about complying with those regulations:

Federal Trade Commision (FTC)
Pennsylvania Ave & 6th St NW
Washington DC 20580

Co-op mailing is combining your mailer with someone else's and then sharing the expenses. This is one way to reduce your mailing costs, but it will dilute your message. Co-op with someone whose product is compatible with yours, to reduce competing or conflicting messages.

❏ **Mailing List Broker.** Below are mailing list brokers who specialize in renting or selling address labels and lists to book publishers. Request list types and pricing information.

Ad-Lib Publications
51-1/2 West Adams
Fairfield IA 52556
(800) 669-0773

American Booksellers Association
560 White Plains Road
Tarrytown NY 10591
(800) 637-0037

Cahners Direct Mail Service
249 West 17th St
New York NY 10011
(800) 537-7930

Para-Lists by Poynter
P.O. Box 4232
Santa Barbara CA 93140
(805) 968-7277

Twin Peaks Mailing Lists
P.O. Box 129
Vancouver WA 9866
(206) 694-2462

❏ **Author's Tours.** Do you like to travel? Does your book have a broad appeal? If so, author's tours can be a rewarding although expensive endurance test, but one of the best ways to reach a large book buying public. Pick the destination(s), and at least 6 weeks in advance, book yourself on as many TV and radio shows as possible. Inform all bookstores (in each area) of your promotional activity encouraging them to have your book in stock. Select the area's most popular bookstore in which to do a lecture or reading and booksigning. Send a notice to the local newspaper outlining your activity, as they may be interested in an interview or at least a mention in their paper. *Keep your wholesaler or distributor current of your plans.*

Tip: Bring extra books in the event the bookstores do not have your book in stock.

❏ **Shipping & Mailing Books.** When shipping pallets of books, use national freight forwarders listed in the phone book. They base their rate on shipping location, weight, and freight class. Paperback books have a different and less expensive freight class than the standard book class rate (class 65 versus 60 respectively). UPS ground offers a fine service for smaller quantities and offers a pick-up service to contracted customers. Single copies can be mailed most economically through the Postal Service at **Book Rate** or the lower **Library Rate** when mailing to Libraries. The Post Office also offers **2 lbs. two-day priority** at a bargain price compared to the overnight express service, providing the extra day delay won't make a difference. Shipping expenses add up quickly, thus it is a good business practice to manage postage and shipping expenses. If you are mailing large quantities on a daily basis, the phone book lists mailing services which specialize in sending bulk quantities.

A Final Note. Publishing and promoting your own book can be an enriching experience. At times things will not run smoothly, and you will ask yourself: *"What did I get myself into?"* Some discouragement can be expected. Meet other self-published authors in your area to pool resources and share experiences. This can be a source of encouragement, a way to shorten the learning curve and combine promotional efforts. Welcome to the world of publishing, and **Good Luck!**

*"The secret to writing a bestseller is simply having a good book
for which there is a need, at the right price,
offered to the right market."*

Subject Index

Index of Organizations and References

Self-Publishing Resources

❑   **A Simple Guide to Self-Publishing**
By Mark Ortman / 60 pages / $5.95

The place to start. This book is filled with time and money-saving tips to print, distribute and promote your own book.

❑   **The Self-Publishing Manual**
By Dan Poynter / 415 pages / $19.95

❑   **The Complete Guide to Self-Publishing**
By Tom & Marilyn Ross / 420 pages / $18.95

Both are very comprehensive and informative books about self-publising. Poynter's book is more thorough, but Ross's book is more readable. Each includes everything you will need to write, publish, promote and sell your own book.

❑   **Book Publishing Resource Guide**
By Marie Kiefer / 378 pages / $25.00

An indispensable resource. This directory includes the names, addresses, phone numbers and key contacts for more than 3000 book marketing channels and 5000 publicity outlets.

❑   **1001 Ways to Market Your Books**
By John Kremer / 544 pages / $19.95

Today's most complete handbook on book marketing featuring ideas, techniques, ways to plan promotions and sell your book.

About the Author

Mark Ortman enjoys his work as a workshop leader, author, composer and publisher. Since 1983, after receiving a Master's Degree in Communication from the University of Denver, he has earned eight national instructor awards for his enthusiastic and inspiring teaching style. Mark's published work includes: *Now That Makes Sense!*, a collection of quote-worthy advice on working, relating and getting along with people; *So Many Ways To Say Thank You*, a gift book; and *Wednesday's Dream*, a musical tape. He also does workshops and personal consultations with authors on how to self-publish.